HILARIOUS JOKES

5

YEAR OLD KIDS

Claim your free gifts!

(My way of saying thank you for your support)

Simply visit **haydenfoxmedia.com**
to receive the following:

- 10 Powerful Dinner Conversations To Create Amazing Kids

- 10 Magical Affirmations To Help Kids Become Unstoppable in Life

(you can also scan this QR code)

This book belongs to

charlie

horsolk

Why don't eggs tell jokes?

They might crack up!

What do you call a bear with no teeth?

A gummy bear!

DID YOU KNOW?

Butterflies taste with their feet.

Brown eyes are the most common.

What has keys but can't open locks?

A piano.

RIDDLES

What is full of holes but still holds water?

A sponge.

She sells seashells by the seashore.

TONGUE TWISTER

KNOCK KNOCK!

Who's there?
Lettuce.
Lettuce who?
Lettuce in, it's cold out here.

Who's there?
Justin.
Justin who?
Justin time to wipe my feet!

Who's there?
Europe.
Europe who?
No, you're a poo!

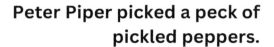

Peter Piper picked a peck of pickled peppers.

What comes down but never goes up?

Rain.

What has a neck but no head?

A bottle.

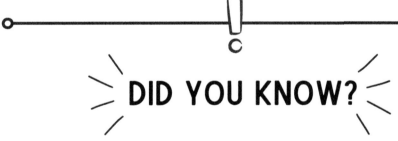

DID YOU KNOW?

The sun is a star at the center of our solar system.

Giraffes have the same number of neck bones as humans: seven.

Why did the teddy bear say no to dessert?

Because she was stuffed.

What do you get when you cross a snowman and a dog?

Frostbite!

DID YOU KNOW?

 **Cranberries bounce like a ball when they are ripe.**

What gets wetter as it dries?

A towel.

What has a face and two hands but no arms or legs?

A clock.

How can a clam cram in a clean cream can?

Who's there?
Atch
Atch who?
Bless you!

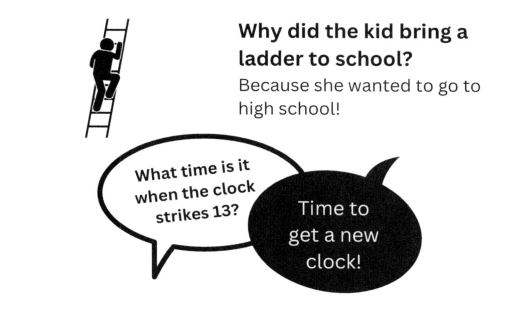

Why did the kid bring a ladder to school?

Because she wanted to go to high school!

What time is it when the clock strikes 13?

Time to get a new clock!

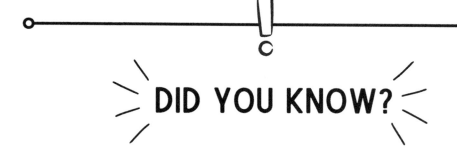

DID YOU KNOW?

Trees can live for thousands of years; some are older than the pyramids.

 Kangaroos can't walk backwards.

I saw Susie sitting in a shoeshine shop.

TONGUE TWISTER

What is so fragile that saying its name breaks it?

Silence.

RIDDLES

What has one eye but can't see?

A needle.

DID YOU KNOW?

The tallest land mammal on Earth is the giraffe.

An octopus has three hearts.

RIDDLES

'What did the pickle say to the other pickle when they fell out of the jar?

Dill with it.

Why did the dinosaur cross the road?

Because the chicken wasn't born yet!'

What is always in front of you but can't be seen?

The future.

What is at the end of a rainbow?

The letter "W".

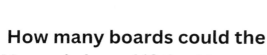

How many boards could the Mongols hoard if the Mongol hordes got bored?

Who's there?
Boo.
Boo who?
Don't cry, it's just a joke!

Why don't some fish play piano?

Because you can't tuna fish!

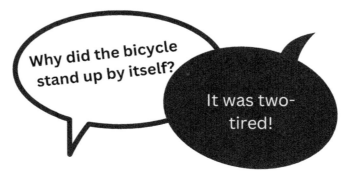

Why did the bicycle stand up by itself?

It was two-tired!

DID YOU KNOW?

Cows have four stomachs to help digest their food.

A group of crows is called a "murder".

Can you can a can as a
canner can can a can?

TONGUE TWISTER

What can travel around the
world while staying in a corner?

A stamp.

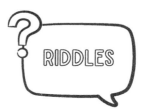
RIDDLES

What can you catch but
not throw?

A cold.

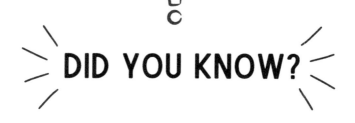

DID YOU KNOW?

Elephants are the only mammals
that can't jump.

Spiders have eight legs.

What do you call a factory that makes okay products?
A satisfactory!

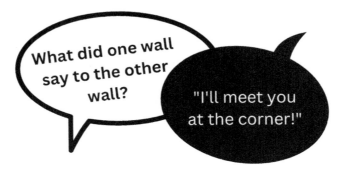

What did one wall say to the other wall?

"I'll meet you at the corner!"

DID YOU KNOW?

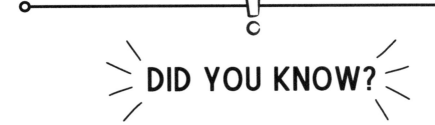

 The heart of a shrimp is located in its head.

A baby kangaroo is called a "joey".

What has a head, a tail, is brown, and has no legs?

A penny.

What gets bigger the more you take away from it?

A hole.

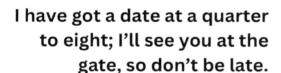

I have got a date at a quarter to eight; I'll see you at the gate, so don't be late.

Who's there?
Olive.
Olive who?
Olive you and I miss you!

Why do we never tell secrets on a farm?

Because the potatoes have eyes and the corn has ears!

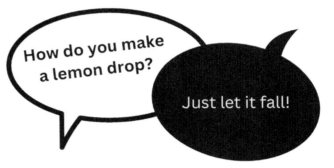

How do you make a lemon drop?

Just let it fall!

DID YOU KNOW?

 Bananas are berries, but strawberries are not.

 A group of jellyfish is called a "smack".

You know New York, you need New York, you know you need unique New York.

What has many keys but can't open a single lock?

A piano.

What has teeth but cannot bite?

A comb.

DID YOU KNOW?

 Frogs absorb water through their skin so they don't need to drink.

Who's there?
Goliath.
Goliath who?
Goliath down, you looketh tired!

Who's there?
Radio.
Radio who?
Radio not, here I come!

What goes up and down but doesn't move?

A staircase.

What can be broken without being held?

A promise.

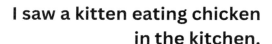

I saw a kitten eating chicken in the kitchen.

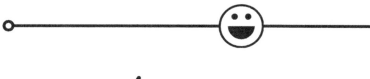

Who's there?
Cow says.
Cow says who?
No, cow says moooo!

Why did the banana go to the doctor?

Because it wasn't peeling well!

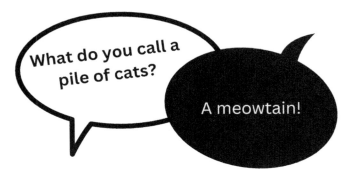

What do you call a pile of cats?

A meowtain!

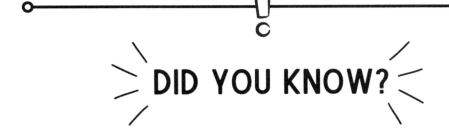

DID YOU KNOW?

 The Great Wall of China is the longest wall in the world.

The world's largest desert is Antarctica, not the Sahara.

If a dog chews shoes, whose shoes does he choose?

TONGUE TWISTER

What has words but never speaks?

A book.

RIDDLES

What runs all around a backyard yet never moves?

A fence.

DID YOU KNOW?

Turtles can breathe through their butts.

Bats are the only mammals that can fly.

What do you call an elephant that doesn't matter?
An irrelephant!

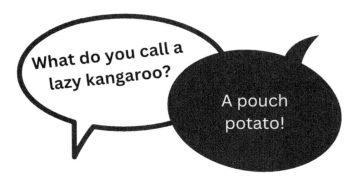

DID YOU KNOW?

 Some cats are allergic to humans.

 The smallest bone in your body is in your ear.

What has many rings but no fingers?

A telephone.

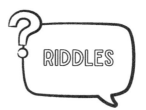

RIDDLES

What has an eye but can't see and is stronger than any man?

A hurricane.

I thought I thought of thinking of thanking you.

TONGUE TWISTER

KNOCK KNOCK!

Who's there?
Harry.
Harry who?
Harry up and answer the door!

What animal is always at a baseball game?

A bat!

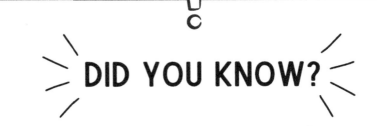

Why don't scientists trust atoms?

Because they make up everything!

DID YOU KNOW?

The Eiffel Tower in France gets a little taller during the summer because the metal expands from the heat.

I wish to wash my Irish wristwatch.

What goes through cities and fields, but never moves?

A road.

What belongs to you, but other people use it more than you do?

Your name.

DID YOU KNOW?

The Roman Empire was one of the greatest empires in human history.

Who's there?

Canoe.

Canoe who?

Canoe help me with my homework?

Who's there?

Mikey.

Mikey who?

Mikey doesn't fit in the keyhole, let me in!

You answer me, although I never ask you questions. What am I?

A telephone.

I shrink smaller every time I take a bath. What am I?

A bar of soap.

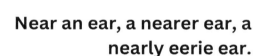

Near an ear, a nearer ear, a nearly eerie ear.

TONGUE TWISTER

KNOCK KNOCK!

Who's there?
Water.
Water who?
Water you waiting for?
Open up!

What do you call a fake noodle?

An impasta!

Why was the belt arrested?

For holding up a pair of pants!

DID YOU KNOW?

A day on Venus is longer than a year on Venus.

You can't hum while holding your nose closed.

Eddie edited it.

What starts with "e" and ends with "e" but only contains one letter?

ɘqoləvnɘ nA

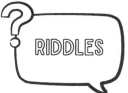

What goes up when rain comes down?

˙ɐllɘɹqɯn nA

DID YOU KNOW?

A crocodile cannot stick its tongue out.

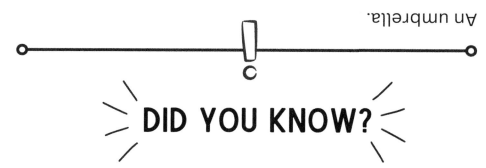

 **What do you call an alligator in a vest?**
An investigator!

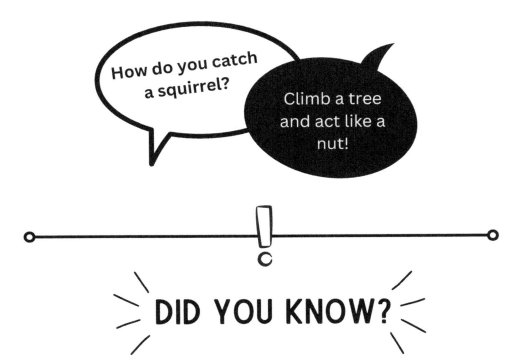

How do you catch a squirrel?

Climb a tree and act like a nut!

DID YOU KNOW?

 Cockroaches can live for a week without their heads!'

 Horses and cows sleep standing up.

What is black when it's clean and white when it's dirty?

A chalkboard.

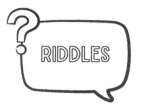

RIDDLES

I'm tall when I'm young, and I'm short when I'm old. What am I?

A candle.

A big black bear sat on a big black rug.

TONGUE TWISTER

KNOCK KNOCK!

Who's there?
Interrupting cow.
Interrup—
MOO!

Why did the computer go to the doctor?

Because it had a virus!

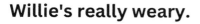

Willie's really weary.

What has a heart that
doesn't beat?

An artichoke.

RIDDLES

What comes once in a minute, twice in a
moment, but never in a thousand years?

The letter "m".

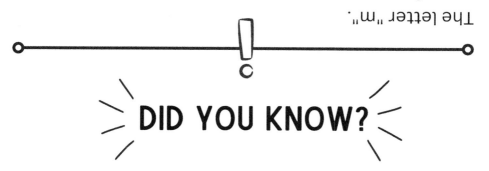

DID YOU KNOW?

The fingerprints of a koala are so
similar to humans that they can be
confused at a crime scene.

What do you get when you cross a cat with a dark horse?

Kitty Perry!

What kind of key opens a banana?

A monkey!

DID YOU KNOW?

Camels have three eyelids to protect themselves from the desert sand.

I have cities but no houses, forests but no trees, and rivers without water. What am I?

A map.

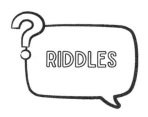

What has a head and a tail but no body?

A coin.

Tom threw Tim three thumbtacks.

TONGUE TWISTER

KNOCK KNOCK!

Who's there?
Howard.
Howard who?
Howard you like to be knocking for a change?

What do you call a boomerang that doesn't work?

A stick!

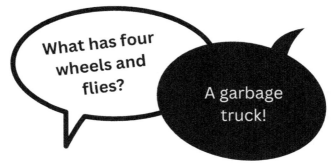

What has four wheels and flies?

A garbage truck!

DID YOU KNOW?

 The opposite sides of a dice cube always add up to seven.

He threw three free throws.

What is as light as a feather, but even the strongest man can't hold it for much more than a minute?

His breath.

RIDDLES

What can be heard but not touched or seen?

Your voice.

DID YOU KNOW?

Bees are found everywhere in the world except Antarctica.

Monkeys can go bald in their old age, just like humans.

How do you organize a space party?

You planet!

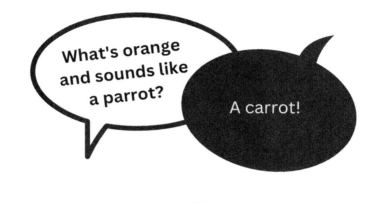

What's orange and sounds like a parrot?

A carrot!

DID YOU KNOW?

The Nile River is the longest river in the world.

The universe is constantly expanding.

I speak without a mouth and hear without ears. I have no body, but I come alive with wind. What am I?

An echo.

RIDDLES

What kind of band never plays music?

A rubber band.

Which wristwatches are Swiss wristwatches?

TONGUE TWISTER

KNOCK KNOCK!

Who's there?
Annie.
Annie who?
Annie thing you can do, I can do too!

What do you get from a pampered cow?

Spoiled milk!

Fine fresh fish for you.

What has a neck but no head, and two arms but no hands?

A shirt.

What has a bottom at the top?

Your legs!

DID YOU KNOW?

Most dinosaurs were herbivores or plant eaters.

Sharks have been around longer than trees.

Why did the girl smear peanut butter on the road?

To go with the traffic jam!

What's a ghost's favorite dessert?

Boo-berries!

DID YOU KNOW?

The highest mountain on Earth is Mount Everest.

Venus is the hottest planet in our solar system.

I am not alive, but I grow; I don't have lungs, but I need air; I don't have a mouth, but water kills me. What am I?

Fire.

RIDDLES

What has a thumb and four fingers but is not alive?

A glove.

Three thin thinkers thinking thick thoughtful thoughts.

TONGUE TWISTER

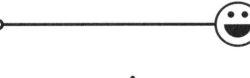

KNOCK KNOCK!

Who's there?
Dishes.
Dishes who?
Dishes a very bad joke!

What do you call a dinosaur with an extensive vocabulary?
A thesaurus!

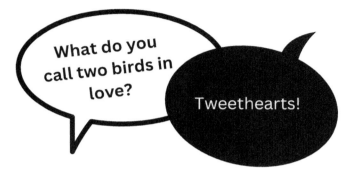

What do you call two birds in love?

Tweethearts!

DID YOU KNOW?

The first person to go to space was Yuri Gagarin.

Octopuses have blue blood.

Betty Botter bought some butter but she said the butter's bitter.

I have keys but no locks. I have space but no room. You can enter but can't go outside. What am I?

A keyboard.

What can be caught but is not a cold?

A yawn.

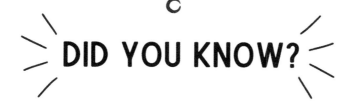

DID YOU KNOW?

There are more stars in the universe than grains of sand on all the beaches on Earth.

Why can't your nose be 12 inches long?

Because then it would be a foot!

How do bees get to school?

By school buzz!

DID YOU KNOW?

The shortest war in history was between Britain and Zanzibar on August 27, 1896. Zanzibar surrendered after 38 minutes.

What has a bed but never sleeps and can run but never walks?

A river.

RIDDLES

Where is today before yesterday?

In a dictionary.

Six sleek swans swam swiftly southwards.

TONGUE TWISTER

Who's there?
Robin.
Robin who?
Robin you! Hand over the candy!

KNOCK KNOCK!

Why don't secret agents sleep?

They're afraid they might spill the beans!

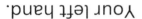

Gobbling gorgoyles gobbled gobbling goblins.

TONGUE TWISTER

What can you hold in your right hand but never in your left hand?

Your left hand.

RIDDLES

I have branches, but no fruit, trunk or leaves. What am I?

A bank.

DID YOU KNOW?

A blue whale's heart is so big that a small child can swim through its arteries.

What's brown and sticky?

A stick!

What do you call a ghost's true love?

His ghoul-friend!

DID YOU KNOW?

 Ants never sleep and don't have lungs.

A group of unicorns is called a blessing.

What goes up but never comes down?

Your age.

RIDDLES

What is cut on a table, but is never eaten?

A deck of cards.

Fred fed Ted bread, and Ted fed Fred bread.

TONGUE TWISTER

KNOCK KNOCK!

Who's there?
Tank.
Tank who?
You're welcome!

What did the big flower say to the little flower?

Hi, bud!

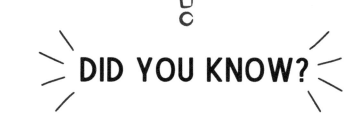

What did the ghost say to the other ghost?

"Do you believe in people?"

DID YOU KNOW?

A bolt of lightning is five times hotter than the sun.

Cats have over 100 vocal sounds, while dogs only have about 10.

I slit the sheet, the sheet I slit, and on the slitted sheet, I sit.

What has many needles, but doesn't sew?

A pine tree.

What has words but never speaks?

A book.

DID YOU KNOW?

The eyes of an ostrich are bigger than its brain.

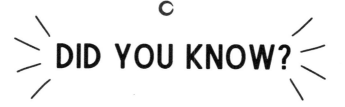

What did the janitor say when he jumped out of the closet?
"Supplies!"

Why don't skeletons fight each other?

They don't have the guts.

DID YOU KNOW?

The smallest bone in the human body is the stirrup bone, which is located in the ear.

I fly without wings. What am I?

Time.

RIDDLES

What question can you never answer "yes" to?

Are you asleep?

A skunk sat on a stump and thunk the stump stunk, but the stump thunk the skunk stunk.

TONGUE TWISTER

KNOCK KNOCK!

Who's there?
Luke.
Luke who?
Luke through the peephole and find out!

What do you call a snowman with a six-pack?

An abdominal snowman!

Lesser leather never weathered wetter weather better.

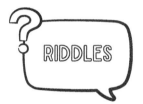

What begins with T, ends with T, and has T in it?

A teapot.

What is always coming but never arrives?

Tomorrow.

DID YOU KNOW?

The tallest tree ever was an Australian eucalyptus – In 1872 it was measured at 435 feet tall.

What do you get when you cross a refrigerator with a radio?

Cool music!

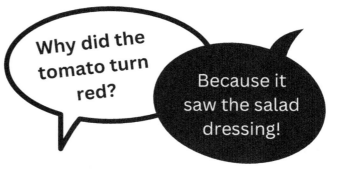

Why did the tomato turn red?

Because it saw the salad dressing!

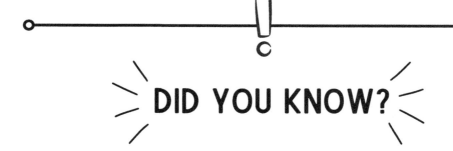

DID YOU KNOW?

The average person walks the equivalent of five times around the world in their lifetime.

I'm where yesterday follows today, and tomorrow's in the middle. What am I?

A dictionary.

RIDDLES

What can fill a room but takes up no space?

Light.

Which witch is which?

TONGUE TWISTER

KNOCK KNOCK!

Who's there?
Ivana.
Ivana who?
Ivana new toy for Christmas!

What do you get when you cross a snake and a pie?

A python!

What do you call an illegally parked frog?

Toad.

DID YOU KNOW?

The word "astronaut" means "star sailor" in its origins.

Water makes up about 71% of the Earth's surface.

Six sticky skeletons.

TONGUE TWISTER

I am taken from a mine, and shut up in a wooden case, from which I am never released, and yet I am used by almost every person. What am I?

RIDDLES

Pencil lead.

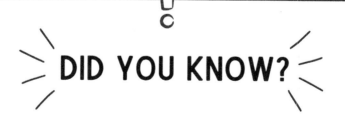

DID YOU KNOW?

A human's nose and ears continue growing throughout their entire life.

How does a cucumber become a pickle?

It goes through a jarring experience!

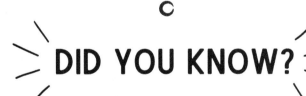

Why don't oysters share their pearls?

Because they're shellfish!

DID YOU KNOW?

The lifespan of a housefly is typically around 30 days.

A baby spider is called a spiderling.

I go in hard, come out soft, and am never the same. What am I?

Gum.

RIDDLES

You walk into a room that contains a match, a kerosene lamp, a candle, and a fireplace. What would you light first?

The match.

Old oily Ollie oils old oily autos.

TONGUE TWISTER

KNOCK KNOCK!

Who's there?
Needle.
Needle who?
Needle little help getting in, it's locked!

Who's there?
Amos.
Amos who?
A mosquito bit me!

Who's there?
Aida.
Aida who?
Aida sandwich for lunch today.

Three free throws.

If you have it, you want to share it. If you share it, you don't have it. What is it?

A secret.

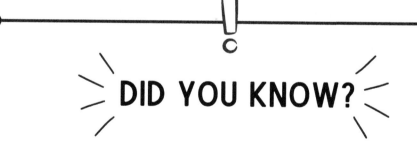

DID YOU KNOW?

Bumblebee bats are the smallest mammals on Earth.

Why do seagulls fly over the sea?

Because if they flew over the bay, they'd be bagels!

What did the zero say to the eight?

Nice belt!

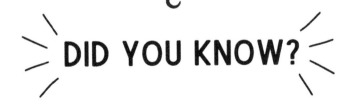

DID YOU KNOW?

You can't sneeze with your eyes open.

Chocolate was once used as currency.

What begins and has no end, and is the ending of all that begins?
Death.

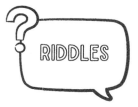

What is as big as an elephant but weighs nothing at all?
The shadow of an elephant.

Red Buick, blue Buick.

Who's there?
Icy.
Icy who?
Icy you, open the door!

What do you call a sleeping bull?

A bulldozer!

Why did the picture go to jail?

Because it was framed!

DID YOU KNOW?

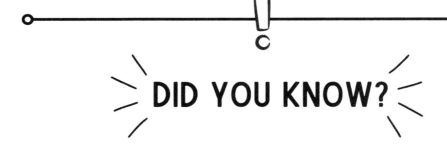

The first tea bags were made of silk.

A group of frogs is called an army.

Real weird rear wheels.

What has a golden head, a golden tail, but no body?

A gold coin.

RIDDLES

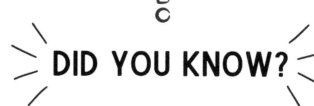

DID YOU KNOW?

Some bamboo plants can grow almost a meter in just one day.

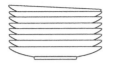

What did one plate say to the other plate?

Dinner's on me!

What do you call a dog that loves to take baths?

A shampoo-dle!

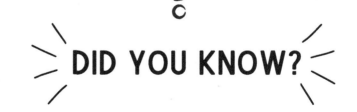

DID YOU KNOW?

The inventor of the light bulb, Thomas Edison, was afraid of the dark.

What can point in every direction but can't reach the destination by itself?

Your finger.

RIDDLES

I'm not alive, but I can die. What am I?

A battery.

Roofs of mushrooms rarely mush too much.

TONGUE TWISTER

KNOCK KNOCK!

Who's there?
Orange.
Orange who?
Orange you going to let me in?

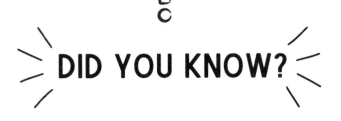

DID YOU KNOW?

The heart of a blue whale is as large as a small car.

The largest animal ever known to have existed is the blue whale.

Who's there?
Doughnut.
Doughnut who?
Doughnut forget to let me in!

Rolling red wagons.

Who's there?
Wooden shoe.
Wooden shoe who?
Wooden shoe like to hear another joke?

How does a scientist freshen her breath?
With experi-mints!

What does a cloud wear under his raincoat?

Thunderwear!

DID YOU KNOW?

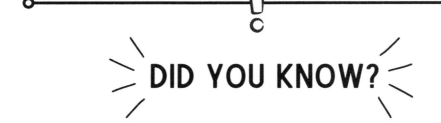

Applesauce was the first food eaten in space by astronauts.'

Fred's friends fried Fritos for Friday's food.

TONGUE TWISTER

What can be cracked, made, told, and played?

A joke.

RIDDLES

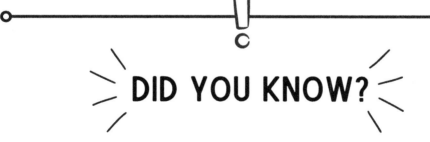

DID YOU KNOW?

There is no sound in outer space!

Why did the golfer bring two pairs of pants?

In case he got a hole in one!

What's a cat's favorite button on the remote?

Paws!

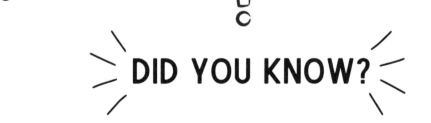

DID YOU KNOW?

'Ice cream once used to be called cream ice.'

Who's there?
Alex.
Alex who?
Alex-plain later, just open the door!

She sees cheese.

Who's there?
Isabel.
Isabel who?
Isabel necessary on a bike?

What did the traffic light say to the car?

Don't look! I'm about to change.

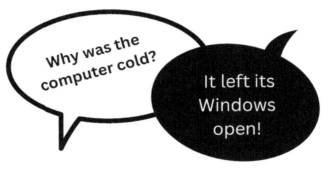

Why was the computer cold?

It left its Windows open!

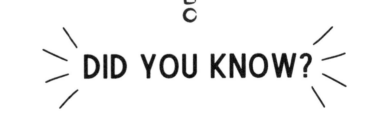

DID YOU KNOW?

The total weight of all ants on Earth is about the same as the weight of all humans.

A big bug bit the little beetle but the little beetle bit the big bug back.

I'm lighter than air but a million men can't lift me. What am I?

A bubble.

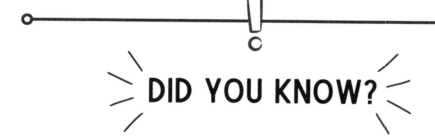

 Honeybees can recognize human faces.

What do you call a dentist who doesn't like tea?

Denis!

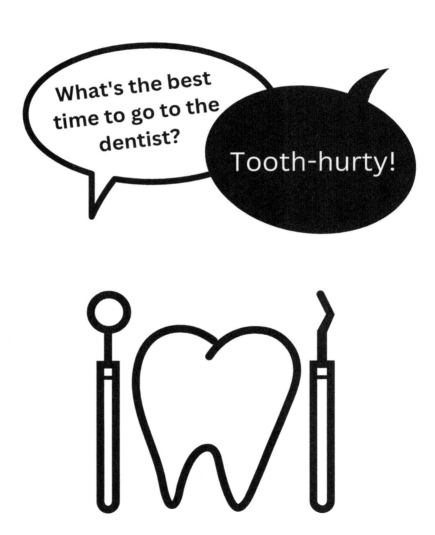

Who's there?
Alpaca.
Alpaca who?
Alpaca the suitcase, you load up the car!

We're real rear wheels.

Who's there?
Art.
Art who?
Art you glad I got great jokes?!

What do you call cheese that isn't yours?

Nacho cheese!

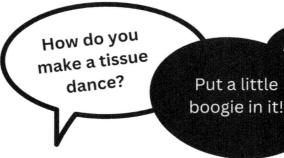

How do you make a tissue dance?

Put a little boogie in it!

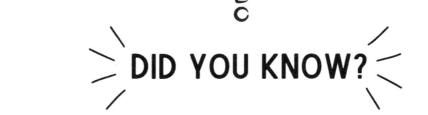

DID YOU KNOW?

A group of owls is called a "parliament".

The Atlantic Ocean is the saltiest of all the oceans.

Black back bat.

What has a mouth but can't chew and runs but cannot walk?

A river.

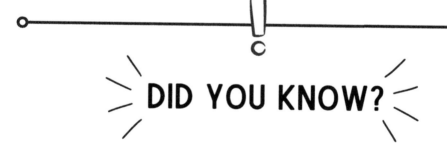

DID YOU KNOW?

A cat has 32 muscles in each ear.

What do you call a book club that's been stuck on one book for months?

A slow readers club!

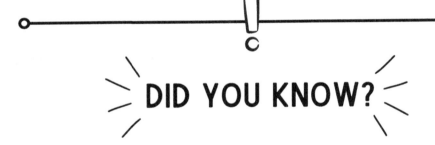

Why do birds fly south for the winter?

Because it's too far to walk!

DID YOU KNOW?

Most of the Earth's oxygen is produced by the ocean.

Eleven benevolent elephants.

What has an eye but can't see
and whistles on a windy day?

A keyhole.

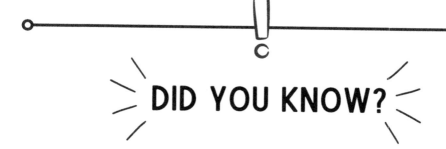

DID YOU KNOW?

The world's largest
snowflake recorded was
15 inches wide.

Why don't skeletons go to scary movies?

They don't have the nerves!

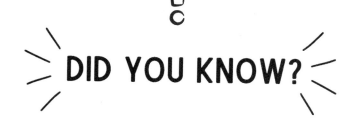

Why do cows have hooves instead of feet?

Because they lactose!

DID YOU KNOW?

An elephant's skin can be one inch thick.

He threw three balls.

I go in dry and come out wet,
the longer I'm in, the stronger it
will get. What am I?

Tea Bag.

RIDDLES

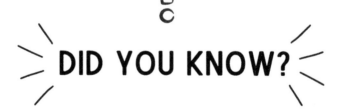
DID YOU KNOW?

 Starfish have no brain
and no blood.

Who's there?
Hal.
Hal who?
Hal will you know if you don't open the door!

Who's there?
Yacht.
Yacht who?
Yacht to know me by now!

Two tried and true tridents.

What building has the most stories?

The library.

DID YOU KNOW?

 The largest known living organism is an aspen grove.

Why did the girl sit on the clock?
She wanted to be on time!

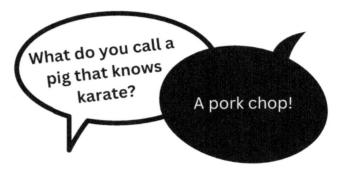

What do you call a pig that knows karate?

A pork chop!

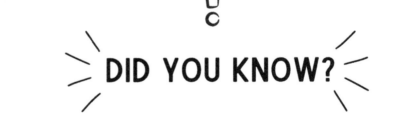

DID YOU KNOW?

A baby has more bones than an adult human because some of the bones fuse over time.

Who's there?
Hugo.
Hugo who?
Hugo your way and I'll go mine.

Quick kiss. Quicker kiss.

Who's there?
June.
June who?
June know any good knock-knock jokes?

What do you call a dinosaur that is sleeping?
A dino-snore!

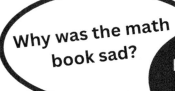

Why was the math book sad?

Because it had too many problems.

DID YOU KNOW?

Dolphins sleep with one eye open.

 Penguins can't fly, but they are excellent swimmers.

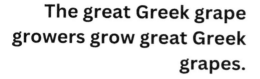

The great Greek grape growers grow great Greek grapes.

What did one volcano say to the other?

I lava you.

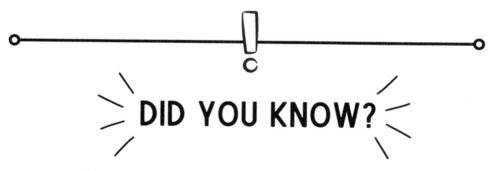

DID YOU KNOW?

The average person laughs about 15 times a day.

How do you stop a bull from charging?
Cancel its credit card!

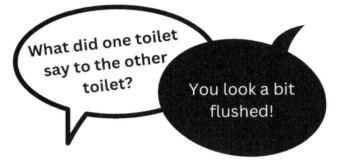

What did one toilet say to the other toilet?

You look a bit flushed!

DID YOU KNOW?

A group of rhinos is called a crash.

Who's there?
Cook.
Cook who?
Cook who's talking now!

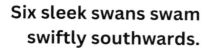

**Six sleek swans swam
swiftly southwards.**

Who's there?
Mustache.
Mustache who?
Mustache you a question,
but I'll shave it for later.

What did the Dalmatian say after dinner?

That hit the spot!

Why did the student eat his homework?

Because his teacher told him it was a piece of cake!

Singing Sammy sung
songs on sinking sand.

What has a tongue, cannot
walk, but gets around a lot?

A shoe.

DID YOU KNOW?

Vatican City is the smallest
city in the world.

What is a cat's favorite color?

Purr-ple!

What kind of tree fits in your hand?

A palm tree!

DID YOU KNOW?

Honey never spoils if it is stored properly.

Snails can sleep for three years without eating.

Giddy gophers greedily gobble gooey goodies.

You can see me in the water, but I never get wet. What am I?

A reflection.

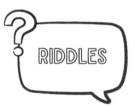

RIDDLES

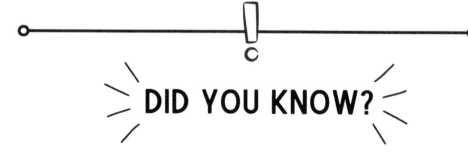

DID YOU KNOW?

It's impossible for most people to lick their own elbow.

What did the shark say after eating a clownfish?

"This tastes a little funny!"

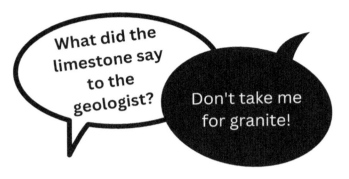

What did the limestone say to the geologist?

Don't take me for granite!

DID YOU KNOW?

The smell of freshly-cut grass is actually a plant distress call.

Wayne went to wales to watch walruses

What can pass in front of the sun without making a shadow?

The wind.

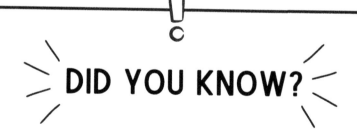

DID YOU KNOW?

Grasshoppers have ears on their bellies.

The Amazon Rainforest produces 20% of the world's oxygen.

Leave Your Feedback on Amazon

Please think about leaving some feedback via a review on Amazon. It may only take a moment, but it really does mean the world for small businesses like mine.

Even if you did not enjoy this title, please let us know the reason(s) in your review so that we may improve this title and serve you better.

From the Publisher

Hayden Fox's mission is to create premium content for children that will help them expand their vocabulary, grow their imaginations, gain confidence, and share tons of laughs along the way.

Without you, however, this would not be possible, so we sincerely thank you for your purchase and for supporting our company mission.

Don't forget your free gifts!

(My way of saying thank you for your support)

Simply visit **haydenfoxmedia.com** to receive the following:

- 10 Powerful Dinner Conversations To Create Amazing Kids

- 10 Magical Affirmations To Help Kids Become Unstoppable in Life

(you can also scan this QR code)

More titles you're sure to love!

HAYDEN FOX

Printed in Great Britain
by Amazon